PREFACE

Learning to play a musical instrument is one of the most satisfying experiences a person can have. Being able to play along with other musicians makes that even more rewarding. This collection of songs is designed to make it easy to enjoy the fun of gathering with friends and family to make music together.

The selections in this book include a wide variety of songs drawn from several generations of popular music. From traditional folk melodies to current favorites, these songs will provide fun opportunities to make music with other players. The music for each song displays the chord diagrams for five instruments: ukulele, baritone ukulele, guitar, mandolin and banjo. The chord diagrams indicate basic, commonly used finger positions. More advanced players can substitute alternate chord formations.

It is easy to find recordings of all of these tunes performed by outstanding musicians. Listening to multiple versions by creative artists can help you to understand the choices you can make about style as you and your friends play these songs.

Arranged by Mark Phillips

ISBN 978-1-5400-4939-1

Visit Hal Leonard Online at
www.halleonard.com

Contact us:
Hal Leonard
7777 West Bluemound Road
Milwaukee, WI 53213
Email: info@halleonard.com

In Europe, contact:
Hal Leonard Europe Limited
42 Wigmore Street
Marylebone, London, W1U 2RN
Email: info@halleonardeurope.com

In Australia, contact:
Hal Leonard Australia Pty. Ltd.
4 Lentara Court
Cheltenham, Victoria, 3192 Australia
Email: info@halleonard.com.au

Standard Ukulele

A   G   D   C   E   Bm

Baritone Ukulele

A   G   D   C   E   Bm

Guitar

A   G   D    C   E   Bm

Mandolin

A   G   D 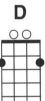   C   E   Bm

Banjo

A   G   D   C   E   Bm

Amie
Words and Music by Craig Fuller

Standard Ukulele

G 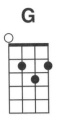 D  Em 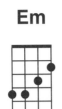 C 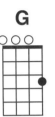 F7 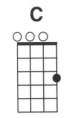 Bm  E7  Am

Baritone Ukulele

G 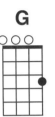 D  Em 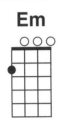 C 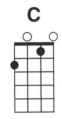 F7  Bm   E7  Am

Guitar

G 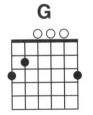 D 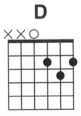 Em 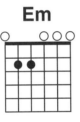 C 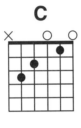 F7  Bm 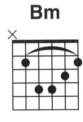 E7 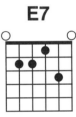 Am

Mandolin

G  D 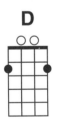 Em  C  F7  Bm 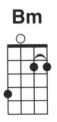 E7  Am

Banjo

G 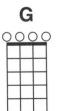 D  Em 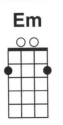 C  F7  Bm  E7 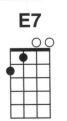 Am

Baby, I Love Your Way

Words and Music by Peter Frampton

Standard Ukulele

G	A7	B7	C	D	D7

Baritone Ukulele

G	A7	B7	C	D	D7

Guitar

G	A7	B7	C	D	D7
		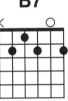	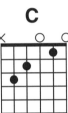		

Mandolin

G	A7	B7	C	D	D7
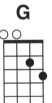		4fr		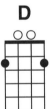	

Banjo

G	A7	B7	C	D	D7

Bad, Bad Leroy Brown

Words and Music by Jim Croce

9

Standard Ukulele

D	G	A
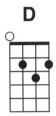		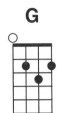

Baritone Ukulele

D	G	A
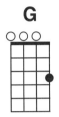	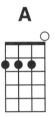	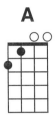

Guitar

D	G	A
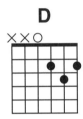	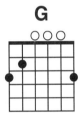	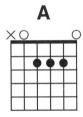

Mandolin

D	G	A
	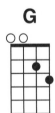	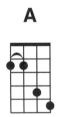

Banjo

D	G	A
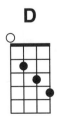	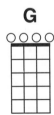	

Blowin' in the Wind

Words and Music by Bob Dylan

Standard Ukulele

G	C	D	Em
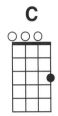 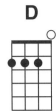  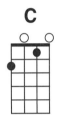 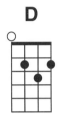 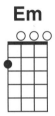 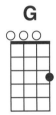

Baritone Ukulele

G	C	D	Em
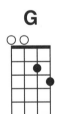   

Guitar

G	C	D	Em
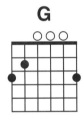 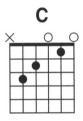 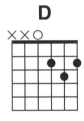 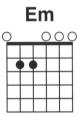

Mandolin

G	C	D	Em
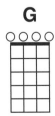   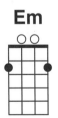

Banjo

G	C	D	Em

Brown Eyed Girl

Words and Music by Van Morrison

Standard Ukulele

Am	G	F	E7sus4	E7	C	Fmaj7
      and

Baritone Ukulele

Am	G	F	E7sus4	E7	C	Fmaj7
    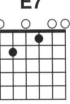 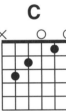

Guitar

Am	G	F	E7sus4	E7	C	Fmaj7

Mandolin

Am	G	F	E7sus4	E7	C	Fmaj7

Banjo

Am	G	F	E7sus4	E7	C	Fmaj7

California Dreamin'
Words and Music by John Phillips and Michelle Phillips

Standard Ukulele

G	C	A7	D7	G7	C#°7	D7#5

Baritone Ukulele

G	C	A7	D7	G7	C#°7	D7#5

Guitar

G	C	A7	D7	G7	C#°7	D7#5
			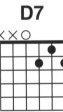			

Mandolin

G	C	A7	D7	G7	C#°7	D7#5

Banjo

G	C	A7	D7	G7	C#°7	D7#5

The Campfire Song Song

from *SPONGEBOB SQUAREPANTS*

Words and Music by Carl Williams, Dan Povenmire, Jay Lender, Michael Culross and Michael Walker

Standard Ukulele

C	F	G	G7
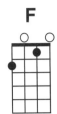   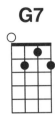

Baritone Ukulele

C	F	G	G7
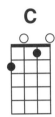 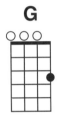 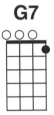 

Guitar

C	F	G	G7
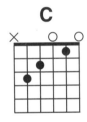 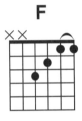 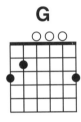 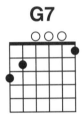

Mandolin

C	F	G	G7
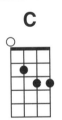 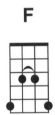 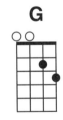 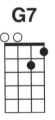

Banjo

C	F	G	G7
  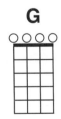 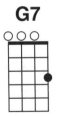

Catch the Wind

Words and Music by Donovan Leitch

Standard Ukulele

D	C	Bm	E	A	Asus4	G
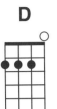	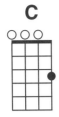		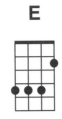	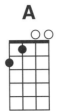	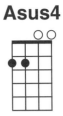	

Baritone Ukulele

D	C	Bm	E	A	Asus4	G
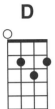		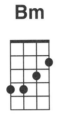				

Guitar

D	C	Bm	E	A	Asus4	G
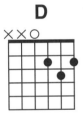	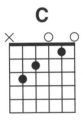	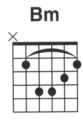			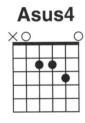	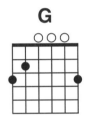

Mandolin

D	C	Bm	E	A	Asus4	G
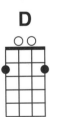	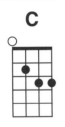	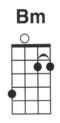		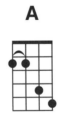	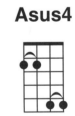	

Banjo

D	C	Bm	E	A	Asus4	G

Danny's Song

Words and Music by Kenny Loggins

Standard Ukulele

G	Am	Bm	C	Em	A7	D	Am7

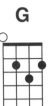 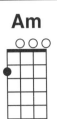  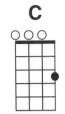 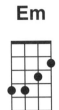 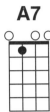  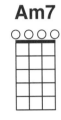

Baritone Ukulele

G	Am	Bm	C	Em	A7	D	Am7

 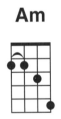 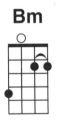 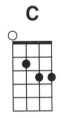  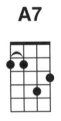  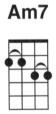

Guitar

G	Am	Bm	C	Em	A7	D	Am7

 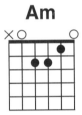 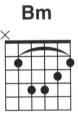 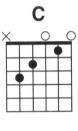  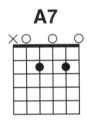 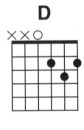 

Mandolin

G	Am	Bm	C	Em	A7	D	Am7

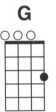       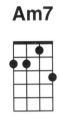

Banjo

G	Am	Bm	C	Em	A7	D	Am7

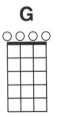       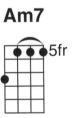

5fr

Daydream Believer

Words and Music by John Stewart

Standard Ukulele

C	F	Dm7	Em	G

Baritone Ukulele

C	F	Dm7	Em	G

Guitar

C	F	Dm7	Em	G

Mandolin

C	F	Dm7	Em	G

Banjo

C	F	Dm7	Em	G

Do You Believe in Magic

Words and Music by John Sebastian

Standard Ukulele

Csus2	Asus2	F	E	G	C	Am

Baritone Ukulele

Csus2	Asus2	F	E	G	C	Am
  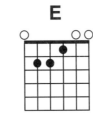  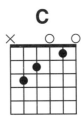  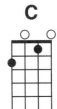   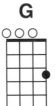 

Guitar

Csus2	Asus2	F	E	G	C	Am
 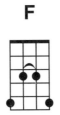  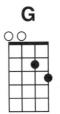 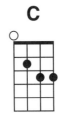 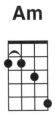

Mandolin

Csus2	Asus2	F	E	G	C	Am
  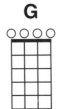 

Banjo

Csus2	Asus2	F	E	G	C	Am

Don't Dream It's Over

Words and Music by Neil Finn

Standard Ukulele

A   **Bm**   **D**

 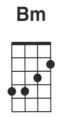 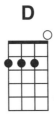

Baritone Ukulele

A   **Bm**   **D**

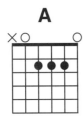 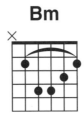 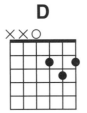

Guitar

A   **Bm**   **D**

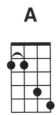 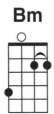 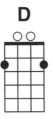

Mandolin

A   **Bm**   **D**

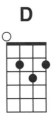

Banjo

A   **Bm**   **D**

  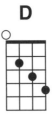

Don't Worry, Be Happy

Words and Music by Bobby McFerrin

Standard Ukulele

C	G	F

Baritone Ukulele

C	G	F
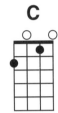	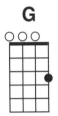	

Guitar

C	G	F
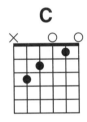	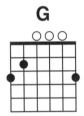	

Mandolin

C	G	F
	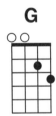	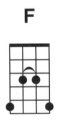

Banjo

C	G	F
	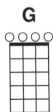	

Down on the Corner
Words and Music by John Fogerty

Verse
Moderately, in 2

1. Ear - ly in the eve - nin' just a - bout sup - per time, __
2. Roos - ter hits the wash - board and peo - ple just got to smile, __
3. You don't need a pen - ny just to hang a - round, __

__ o - ver by the court - house they're
__ Blink - y thumps the gut __ house bass and
__ but if you've got a nick - el, won't you

start - ing to un - wind. __ Four kids on the cor -
so - los for a while. __ Poor - boy twangs the rhy -
lay your mon - ey down? __ O - ver on the cor -

- ner try - na bring you up. __ Wil - ly picks __ a tune __
- thm out on his Kal - a - ma - zoo. __ Wil - ly goes __ in - to __
- ner there's a hap - py noise. __ Peo - ple come __ from all __

__ out and he blow it on the harp. __
__ a dance and dou - bles on ka - zoo. __
__ a - round to watch the mag - ic boy. __

Chorus

Down on the cor - ner, out in the street, __ Wil - ly and the

Poor - boys are play - in'. Bring a nick - el; tap your feet. __

Play 3 times

Standard Ukulele

C	G7	F	Am7	Dm7	D7	C7	Fm
		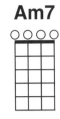					

Baritone Ukulele

C	G7	F	Am7	Dm7	D7	C7	Fm
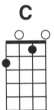							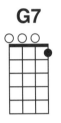

Guitar

C	G7	F	Am7	Dm7	D7	C7	Fm
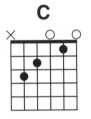	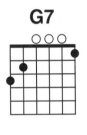	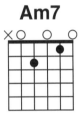					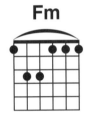

Mandolin

C	G7	F	Am7	Dm7	D7	C7	Fm
	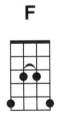	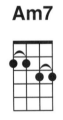				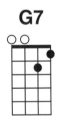	

Banjo

C	G7	F	Am7	Dm7	D7	C7	Fm
		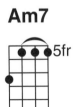 5fr	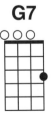				

Edelweiss

from THE SOUND OF MUSIC
Lyrics by Oscar Hammerstein II
Music by Richard Rodgers

Standard Ukulele

G	D	C	Am	Em	Bm

Baritone Ukulele

G	D	C	Am	Em	Bm
					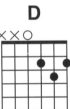

Guitar

G	D	C	Am	Em	Bm

Mandolin

G	D	C	Am	Em	Bm
	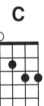				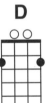

Banjo

G	D	C	Am	Em	Bm
	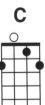				

Father and Son
Words and Music by Cat Stevens

Standard Ukulele

A	Em7	D	E	G5(maj7)	Bm7	G	A7sus2
			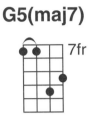				

Baritone Ukulele

A	Em7	D	E	G5(maj7)	Bm7	G	A7sus2
		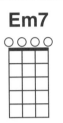	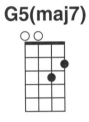			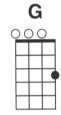	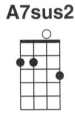

Guitar

A	Em7	D	E	G5(maj7)	Bm7	G	A7sus2
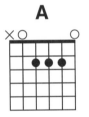	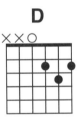				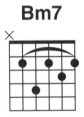	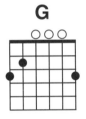	

Mandolin

A	Em7	D	E	G5(maj7)	Bm7	G	A7sus2
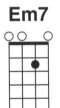	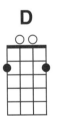						

Banjo

A	Em7	D	E	G5(maj7)	Bm7	G	A7sus2
	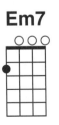			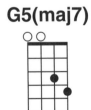		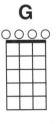	

Fire and Rain

Words and Music by James Taylor

Standard Ukulele

E	A	B7

Baritone Ukulele

E	A	B7

Guitar

E	A	B7

Mandolin

E	A	B7
	4fr	

Banjo

E	A	B7

Folsom Prison Blues

Words and Music by John R. Cash

Standard Ukulele

E   A   D

Baritone Ukulele

E   A   D

Guitar

E   A    D

Mandolin

E   A   D

Banjo

E   A   D

For What It's Worth

Words and Music by Stephen Stills

Verse
Moderately

1. There's some-thing hap-pen-ing here, _____ but what it
2., 3., 4. *See additional lyrics*

is ain't ex - act - ly clear. _ There's a man with a gun o - ver there _

_ tell-ing me I've got to be - ware. _ I think it's time we

stop; chil - dren, what's that sound? _ Ev - 'ry - bod - y look what's go - ing down. _____

Fine

_

Additional Lyrics

2. There's battle lines being drawn.
   Nobody's right if everybody's wrong.
   Young people speaking their minds,
   Getting so much resistance from behind.
   I think it's time we stop; hey, what's that sound?
   Everybody look what's going down.

3. What a field day for the heat.
   A thousand people in the street,
   Singing songs and carrying signs,
   Mostly say, "Hooray for our side."
   It's time we stop; hey, what's that sound?
   Everybody look what's going down.

4. Paranoia strikes deep.
   Into your life it will creep.
   It starts when you're always afraid.
   You step out of line, the man come and take you away.
   We better stop; hey, what's that sound?
   Everybody look what's going down.

Standard Ukulele

E	Asus2	Bsus4

Baritone Ukulele

E	Asus2	Bsus4

Guitar

E	Asus2	Bsus4

Mandolin

E	Asus2	Bsus4

Banjo

E	Asus2	Bsus4

Free Fallin'

Words and Music by Tom Petty and Jeff Lynne

Standard Ukulele

C	F	Dm	B♭	G	Em	Am
		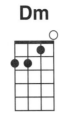		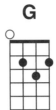		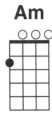

Baritone Ukulele

C	F	Dm	B♭	G	Em	Am
			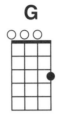	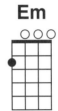	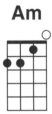	

Guitar

C	F	Dm	B♭	G	Em	Am
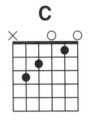	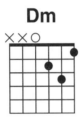	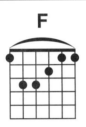	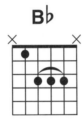			

Mandolin

C	F	Dm	B♭	G	Em	Am
	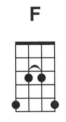			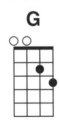		

Banjo

C	F	Dm	B♭	G	Em	Am
		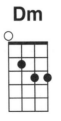		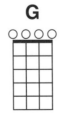	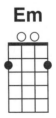	

God Bless the U.S.A.

Words and Music by Lee Greenwood

Standard Ukulele

G	C	D	Em
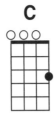	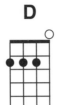	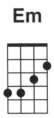	

Baritone Ukulele

G	C	D	Em
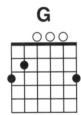	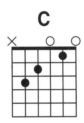	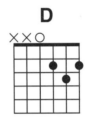	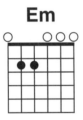

Guitar

G	C	D	Em
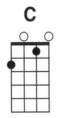		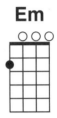	

Mandolin

G	C	D	Em
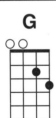		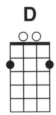	

Banjo

G	C	D	Em
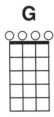			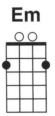

Good Riddance
(Time of Your Life)

Words by Billie Joe
Music by Green Day

Standard Ukulele

C	Am	F	G	Em
		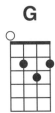		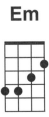

Baritone Ukulele

C	Am	F	G	Em
		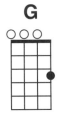		

Guitar

C	Am	F	G	Em
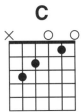		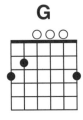		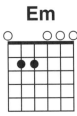

Mandolin

C	Am	F	G	Em
	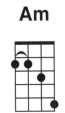		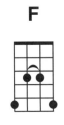	

Banjo

C	Am	F	G	Em
			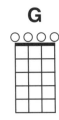	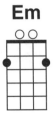

Hallelujah

Words and Music by Leonard Cohen

Standard Ukulele

C 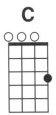 G 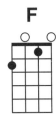 F 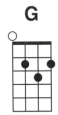 Am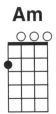

Baritone Ukulele

C 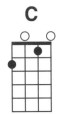 G  F 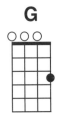 Am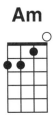

Guitar

C 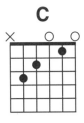 G  F 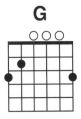 Am

Mandolin

C 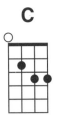 G  F  Am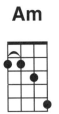

Banjo

C  G 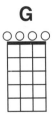 F  Am

Have You Ever Seen the Rain?

Words and Music by John Fogerty

Standard Ukulele

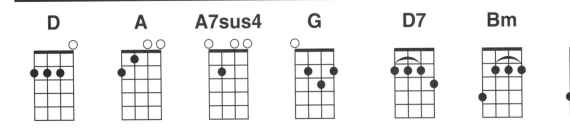

Baritone Ukulele

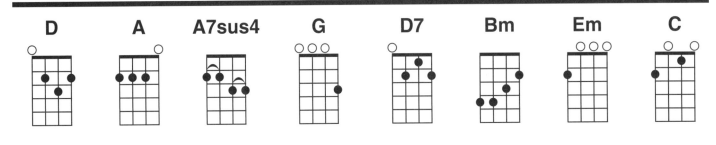

Guitar

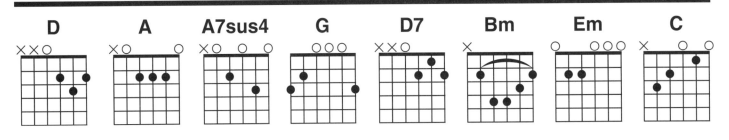

Mandolin

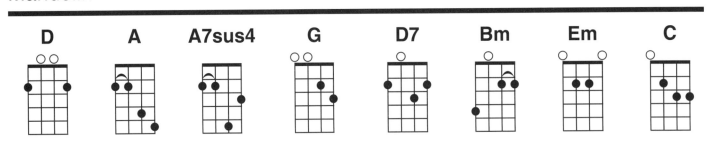

Banjo

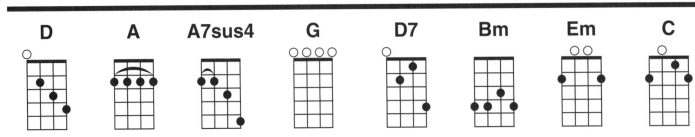

Hey Jude

Words and Music by John Lennon and Paul McCartney

Standard Ukulele

Em   **D6**

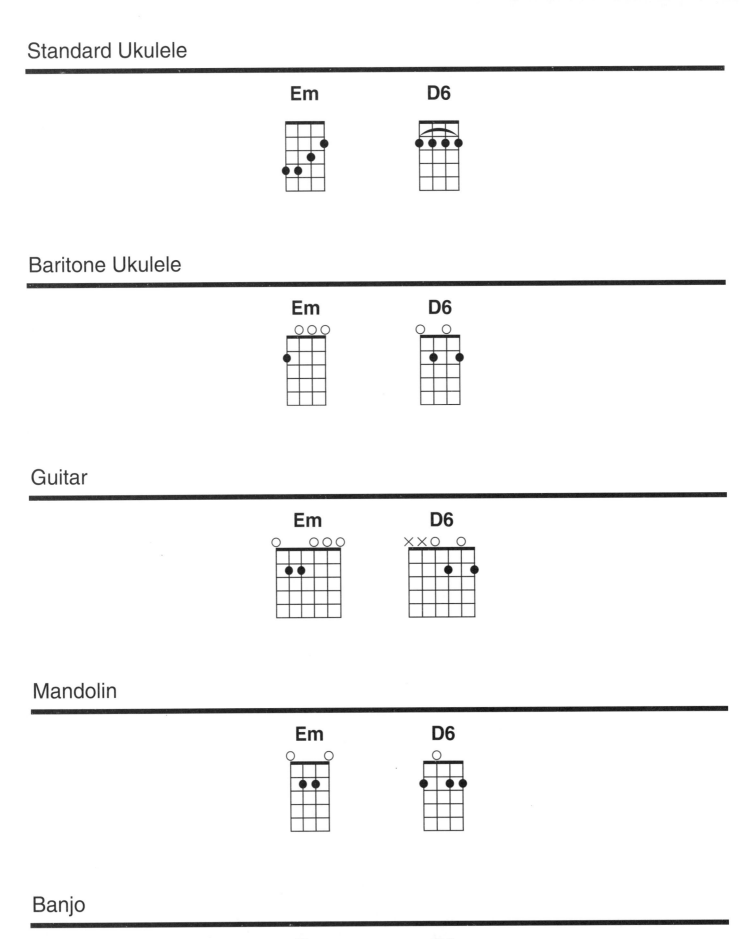

Baritone Ukulele

Em   **D6**

Guitar

Em   **D6**

Mandolin

Em   **D6**

Banjo

Em   **D6**

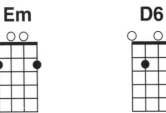

A Horse with No Name

Words and Music by Dewey Bunnell

Standard Ukulele

Am   **C**   **D**   **F**   **E**

Baritone Ukulele

Am   **C**   **D**   **F**   **E**

Guitar

Am   **C** 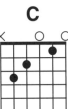 **D**   **F**  **E**

Mandolin

Am   **C**   **D**   **F**   **E**

Banjo

Am   **C**   **D**   **F**   **E**

The House of the Rising Sun
Words and Music by Alan Price

Verse
Slowly, in 2

Additional Lyrics

2. My mother was a tailor, sewed my new blue jeans.
   My father was a gamblin' man down in New Orleans.

3. Now, the only thing a gambler needs is a suitcase and a trunk.
   And the only time he'll be satisfied is when he's all a drunk.

4. Oh mother, tell your children not to do what I have done:
   Spend your lives in sin and misery in the House of the Rising Sun.

5. Well, I've got one foot on the platform, the other on the train.
   And I'm goin' back to New Orleans to wear that ball and chain.

6. Well, there is a house in New Orleans they call the Rising Sun.
   And it's been the ruin of many a poor boy, and God, I know I'm one.

Standard Ukulele

B7	E	A
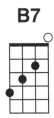		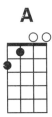

Baritone Ukulele

B7	E	A
	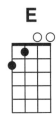	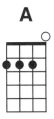

Guitar

B7	E	A
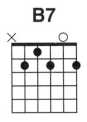	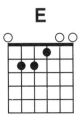	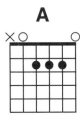

Mandolin

B7	E	A
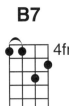	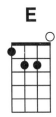	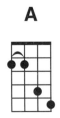

Banjo

B7	E	A
	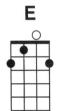	

I Walk the Line

Words and Music by John R. Cash

Standard Ukulele

G	D	C	G7	F

Baritone Ukulele

G	D	C	G7	F

Guitar

G	D	C	G7	F

Mandolin

G	D	C	G7	F

Banjo

G	D	C	G7	F

I'm a Believer

Words and Music by Neil Diamond

Standard Ukulele

C	F	Am	Dm7	G	G7	E7
	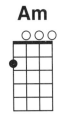		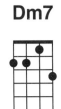	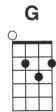	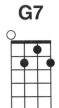	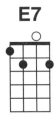

Baritone Ukulele

C	F	Am	Dm7	G	G7	E7
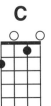					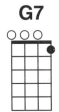	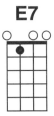

Guitar

C	F	Am	Dm7	G	G7	E7
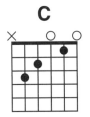	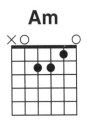	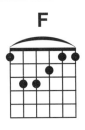			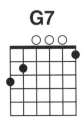	

Mandolin

C	F	Am	Dm7	G	G7	E7
	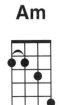				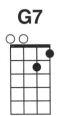	

Banjo

C	F	Am	Dm7	G	G7	E7
				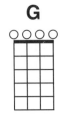		

Imagine

Words and Music by John Lennon

Standard Ukulele

A	E	F♯m	A7	D	Dm	G	B
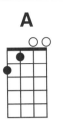			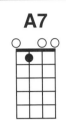	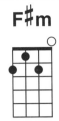	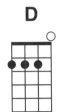		

Baritone Ukulele

A	E	F♯m	A7	D	Dm	G	B
	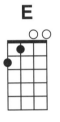	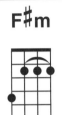			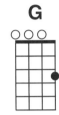		

Guitar

A	E	F♯m	A7	D	Dm	G	B
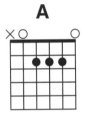			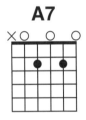				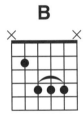

Mandolin

A	E	F♯m	A7	D	Dm	G	B
			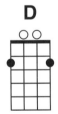	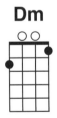		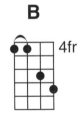	

Banjo

A	E	F♯m	A7	D	Dm	G	B
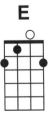	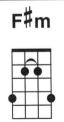				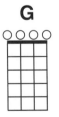		

In My Life

Words and Music by John Lennon and Paul McCartney

Standard Ukulele

Em   Am   D   G   C

Baritone Ukulele

Em   Am   D   G   C

Guitar

Em   Am   D    G   C

Mandolin

Em   Am   D   G 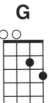   C

Banjo

Em   Am   D   G   C

Island in the Sun
Words and Music by Rivers Cuomo

Standard Ukulele

D	G	A7
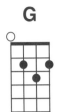	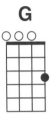	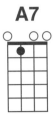

Baritone Ukulele

D	G	A7
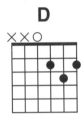	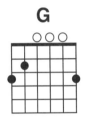	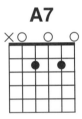

Guitar

D	G	A7
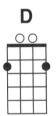	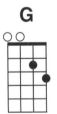	

Mandolin

D	G	A7

Banjo

D	G	A7
	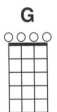	

Jamaica Farewell
Words and Music by Irving Burgie

Standard Ukulele

G	C	D
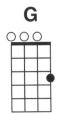	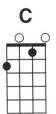	

Baritone Ukulele

G	C	D
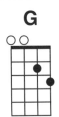		

Guitar

G	C	D
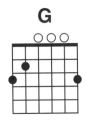	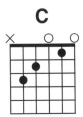	

Mandolin

G	C	D
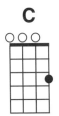	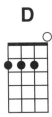	

Banjo

G	C	D
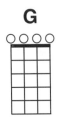		

The Joker

Words and Music by Steve Miller, Eddie Curtis and Ahmet Ertegun

Additional Lyrics

2. People talk about me, baby,
   Say I'm doin' you wrong, doin' you wrong.
   But don't you worry, baby, don' worry,
   'Cause I'm right here, right here, right here,
   Right here at home.

3. You're the cutest thing that I ever did see;
   I really love your peaches, want to shake your tree.
   Lovey dovey, lovey dovey, lovey dovey all the time;
   Ooh wee, baby, I'll sure show you a good time.

Standard Ukulele

G	D	Am	C
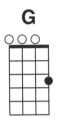 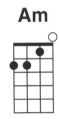  

Baritone Ukulele

G	D	Am	C
 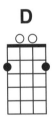 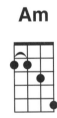 

Guitar

G	D	Am	C
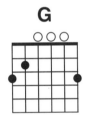 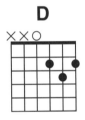  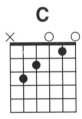

Mandolin

G	D	Am	C
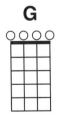   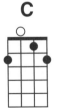

Banjo

G	D	Am	C
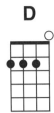 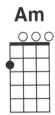 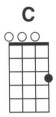

Knockin' on Heaven's Door
Words and Music by Bob Dylan

Verse
Moderately slow

1. Ma - ma, take this badge _____ off of me. _____
2. Ma - ma, put my guns _____ in the ground. _

I cant use it an - y - more. _____
I can't shoot them _____ an - y - more. _____

It's get - tin' dark, _ too dark _ to see. _____
That long black cloud _ is com - in' down. _

I feel I'm knock - in" on heav - en's door. _____

Chorus

Knock, knock, knock - in' on heav - en's door. _____

Knock, knock, knock - in' on heav - en's door. _____

Knock, knock, knock - in' on heav - en's door. _____

Knock, knock, knock - in' on heav - en's door. _

Standard Ukulele

D	G	A
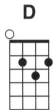	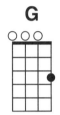	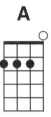

Baritone Ukulele

D	G	A
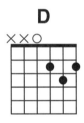	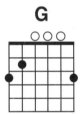	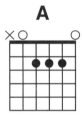

Guitar

D	G	A
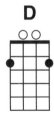	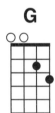	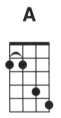

Mandolin

D	G	A
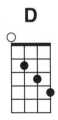	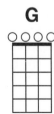	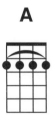

Banjo

D	G	A
	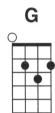	

Kumbaya

Congo Folksong

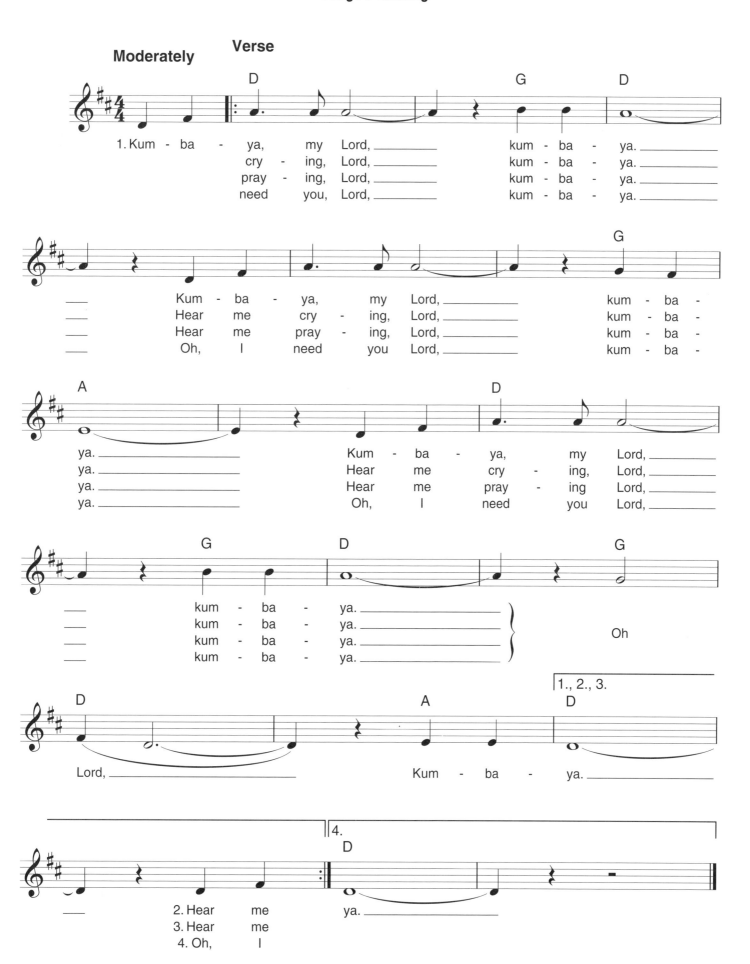

Standard Ukulele

C	Dm	Em	F	G6	G7
			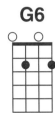	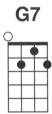	

Baritone Ukulele

C	Dm	Em	F	G6	G7
			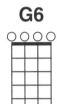	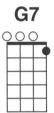	

Guitar

C	Dm	Em	F	G6	G7
	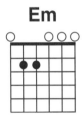		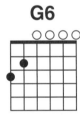		

Mandolin

C	Dm	Em	F	G6	G7
		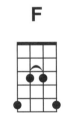	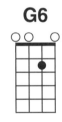	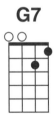	

Banjo

C	Dm	Em	F	G6	G7
			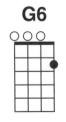	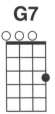	

Lean on Me

Words and Music by Bill Withers

Standard Ukulele

G 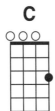   C 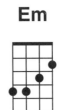   Em 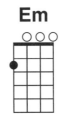   D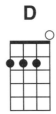

Baritone Ukulele

G 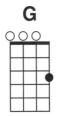   C    Em    D

Guitar

G 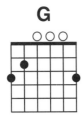   C 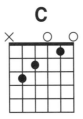   Em 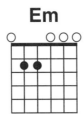   D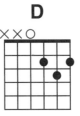

Mandolin

G 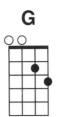   C    Em    D

Banjo

G 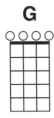   C    Em    D

Leaving on a Jet Plane

Words and Music by John Denver

Standard Ukulele

C	G	Am	F
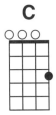	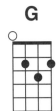	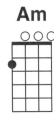	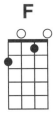

Baritone Ukulele

C	G	Am	F
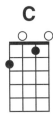	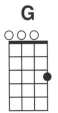	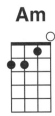	

Guitar

C	G	Am	F
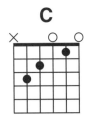	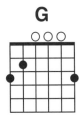		

Mandolin

C	G	Am	F
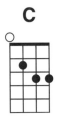	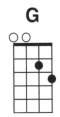		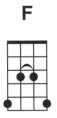

Banjo

C	G	Am	F
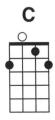	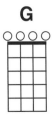		

Let It Be

Words and Music by John Lennon and Paul McCartney

Standard Ukulele

G 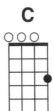   C 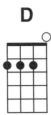   D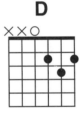

Baritone Ukulele

G    C 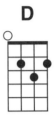   D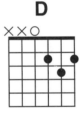

Guitar

G 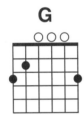   C 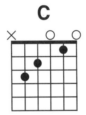   D

Mandolin

G 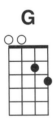   C 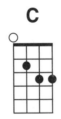   D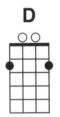

Banjo

G 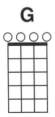   C    D

The Lion Sleeps Tonight

New Lyrics and Revised Music by George David Weiss, Hugo Peretti and Luigi Creatore

Standard Ukulele

D	C	G	Am	Bm

Baritone Ukulele

D	C	G	Am	Bm

Guitar

D	C	G	Am	Bm
	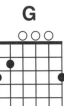			

Mandolin

D	C	G	Am	Bm

Banjo

D	C	G	Am	Bm

Maggie May

Words and Music by Rod Stewart and Martin Quittenton

Verse
Moderately

1. Wake up, Mag - gie, I think I got some-thing to say to you. ___ It's
late Sep - tem-ber and I real - ly should ___ be back ___ at school. I
know I keep you a - mused, ___ but I feel I'm be-ing used. Oh
Mag-gie, I could-n't have tried ___ an - y more. ___ You
led me a - way from home just to save you from be- ing a - lone. You
stole my heart ___ and that's ___ what real - ly hurts. ___

Play 4 times

Additional Lyrics

2. The morning sun when it's in your face really shows your age.
   But that don't worry me none; in my eyes you're everything.
   I laughed at all of your jokes; my love you didn't need to coax.
   Oh Maggie, I couldn't have tried any more.
   You lured me away from home just to save you from being alone.
   You stole my soul and that's a pain I can do without.

3. All I needed was a friend to lend a guiding hand.
   But you turned into a lover, and, mother, what a lover! You wore me out.
   All you did was wreck my bed, and in the morning kick me in the head.
   Oh Maggie, I couldn't have tried anymore.
   You led me away from home 'cause you didn't want to be alone.
   You stole my heart; I couldn't leave you if I tried.

4. I suppose I could collect my books and get on back to school,
   Or steal my daddy's cue and make a living out of playing pool,
   Or find myself a rock 'n' roll band that needs a helping hand.
   Oh Maggie, I wish I'd never seen your face.
   You made a first-class fool out of me, but I'm as blind as a fool can be.
   You stole my heart, but I love you anyway.

Standard Ukulele

C	F	Em	Dm	G7
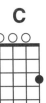			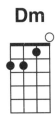	

Baritone Ukulele

C	F	Em	Dm	G7
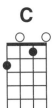				

Guitar

C	F	Em	Dm	G7
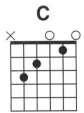	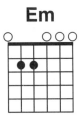			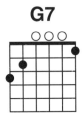

Mandolin

C	F	Em	Dm	G7
	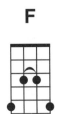		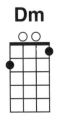	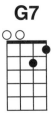

Banjo

C	F	Em	Dm	G7
		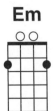		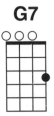

Michael Row the Boat Ashore

Traditional Folksong

Standard Ukulele

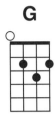 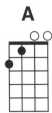 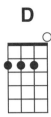

Baritone Ukulele

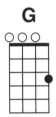  

Guitar

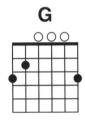 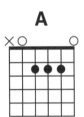 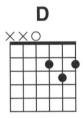

Mandolin

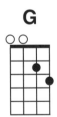 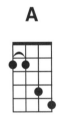 

Banjo

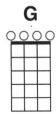  

Mr. Tambourine Man
Words and Music by Bob Dylan

Standard Ukulele

Em	D	C	G	F	A
	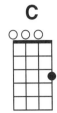				

Baritone Ukulele

Em	D	C	G	F	A
	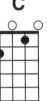				

Guitar

Em	D	C	G	F	A

Mandolin

Em	D	C	G	F	A
		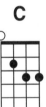		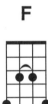	

Banjo

Em	D	C	G	F	A

Nights in White Satin

Words and Music by Justin Hayward

Standard Ukulele

G  **D** 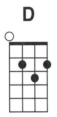 **C**  **Em**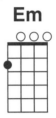

Baritone Ukulele

G 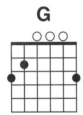 **D** 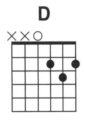 **C** 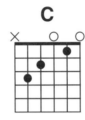 **Em**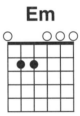

Guitar

G 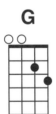 **D**  **C** 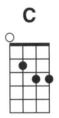 **Em**

Mandolin

G 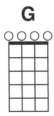 **D**  **C**  **Em**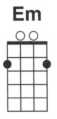

Banjo

G 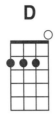 **D** 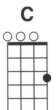 **C**  **Em**

Ob-La-Di, Ob-La-Da

Words and Music by John Lennon and Paul McCartney

Standard Ukulele

F	C	G
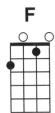	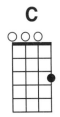	

Baritone Ukulele

F	C	G
	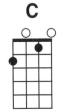	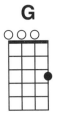

Guitar

F	C	G
	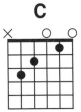	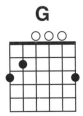

Mandolin

F	C	G
		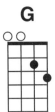

Banjo

F	C	G
	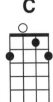	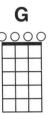

On Top of Spaghetti

Words and Music by Tom Glazer

Standard Ukulele

D	G	A	Em	Dsus4

Baritone Ukulele

D	G	A	Em	Dsus4

Guitar

D	G	A	Em	Dsus4

Mandolin

D	G	A	Em	Dsus4
	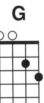			

Banjo

D	G	A	Em	Dsus4

Peaceful Easy Feeling

Words and Music by Jack Tempchin

Standard Ukulele

D	A	Bm	C	G	F

Baritone Ukulele

D	A	Bm	C	G	F

Guitar

D	A	Bm	C	G	F
			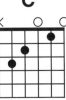		

Mandolin

D	A	Bm	C	G	F
				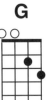	

Banjo

D	A	Bm	C	G	F

Proud Mary

Words and Music by John Fogerty

Standard Ukulele

G	Bm	C	Em	A	D

Baritone Ukulele

G	Bm	C	Em	A	D

Guitar

G	Bm	C	Em	A	D

   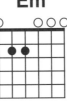 

Mandolin

G	Bm	C	Em	A	D

Banjo

G	Bm	C	Em	A	D

Puff the Magic Dragon

Words and Music by Lenny Lipton and Peter Yarrow

Standard Ukulele

G	Em	C	Am	D

Baritone Ukulele

G	Em	C	Am	D

Guitar

G	Em	C	Am	D
	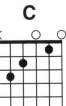			

Mandolin

G	Em	C	Am	D
	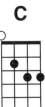	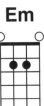		

Banjo

G	Em	C	Am	D

Redemption Song

Words and Music by Bob Marley

Standard Ukulele

G	C	D7
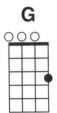		

Baritone Ukulele

G	C	D7
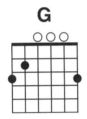	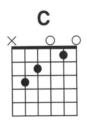	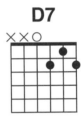

Guitar

G	C	D7
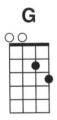		

Mandolin

G	C	D7
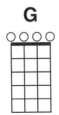		

Banjo

G   C   D7

Ring of Fire

Words and Music by Merle Kilgore and June Carter

Standard Ukulele

G	C	D	Am	A7

Baritone Ukulele

G	C	D	Am	A7

Guitar

G	C	D	Am	A7

Mandolin

G	C	D	Am	A7
	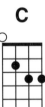	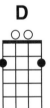		

Banjo

G	C	D	Am	A7

Ripple

Words by Robert Hunter
Music by Jerry Garcia

Additional Lyrics

2. It's a hand-me-down; the thoughts are broken.
   Perhaps they're better left unsung.
   I don't know, don't really care.
   Let there be songs to fill the air.

3. Reach out your hand if your cup be empty.
   If your cup is full, may it be again.
   Let it be known there is a fountain
   That was not made by the hands of men.

4. There is a road, no simple highway
   Between the dawn and the dark of night.
   And if you go, no one may follow.
   That path is for your steps alone.

5. You who choose to lead must follow,
   But if you fall, you fall alone.
   If you should stand, then who's to guide you?
   If I knew the way, I would take you home.

Standard Ukulele

Em	D	G	A

Baritone Ukulele

Em	D	G	A
	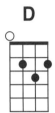	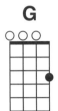	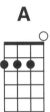

Guitar

Em	D	G	A

Mandolin

Em	D	G	A

Banjo

Em	D	G	A

Scarborough Fair

Traditional English

1. Are you go - ing to Scar - bor - ough Fair?
2. Have her make me a cam - bric shirt,
3. Have her wash it in yon - der well,
4. Have her find me an a - cre of land,
5. Plow the land with the horn of a lamb,

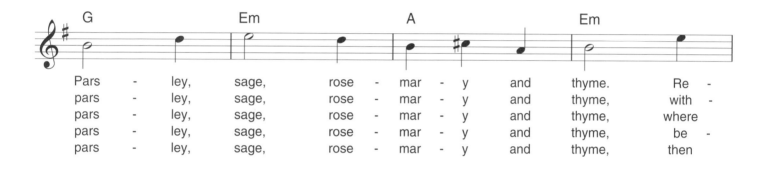

Pars - ley, sage, rose - mar - y and thyme. Re -
pars - ley, sage, rose - mar - y and thyme, with -
pars - ley, sage, rose - mar - y and thyme, where
pars - ley, sage, rose - mar - y and thyme, be -
pars - ley, sage, rose - mar - y and thyme, then

mem - ber me to one who lives there, _____ for
out a seam or fine nee - dle - work, _____ and
ne'er a drop of wa - ter e'er fell, _____ and
tween the sea and o - ver the land, _____ and
sow some seeds from north of the dam, _____ and

Play 5 times

she once was a true love of mine.
then she'll be a true love of mine.
she shall be a true love of mine.
then she'll be a true love of mine.
then she'll be a true love of mine.

Standard Ukulele

  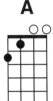

G   B   C   A   E   D   F

  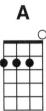

Baritone Ukulele

G   B   C   A   E   D   F

  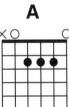  

Guitar

G   B   C   A   E   D   F

Mandolin

G   B   C   A   E   D   F

4fr

  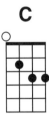 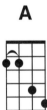

Banjo

G   B   C   A   E   D   F

110

(Sittin' On) The Dock of the Bay

Words and Music by Steve Cropper and Otis Redding

Standard Ukulele

G	Am	F	C
	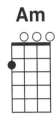	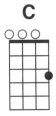	

Baritone Ukulele

G	Am	F	C
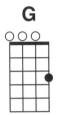	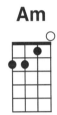		

Guitar

G	Am	F	C
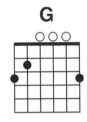	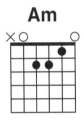		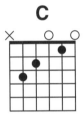

Mandolin

G	Am	F	C
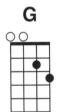	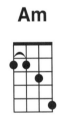	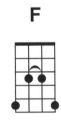	

Banjo

G	Am	F	C
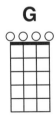			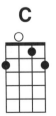

The Sound of Silence

Words and Music by Paul Simon

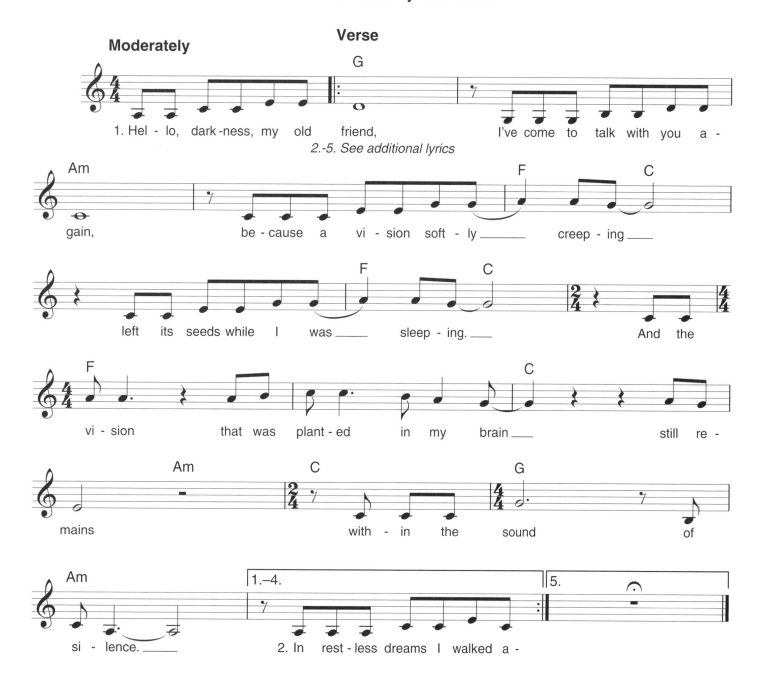

Additional Lyrics

2. In restless dreams I walked alone,
Narrow streets of cobblestone.
'Neath the halo of a streetlamp,
I turned my collar to the cold and damp,
When my eyes were stabbed by the flash
Of a neon light
That split the night and touched the
Sound of silence.

3. And in the naked light I saw
Ten thousand people, maybe more.
People talking without speaking,
People hearing without listening,
People writing songs that voices never share,
And no one dare disturb the sound of silence.

4. "Fools!" said I, "You do not know.
Silence like a cancer grows.
Hear my words that I might teach you.
Take my arms that I might reach you."
But my words, like silent raindrops fell
And echoed in the wells of silence.

5. And the people bowed and prayed
To the neon god they made.
And the sign flashed out its warning
In the words that it was forming.
And the sign said, "The words of the
Prophets are
Written on the subway walls and
Tenement halls."
Whisper the sounds of silence.

Standard Ukulele

G	Em	C	D
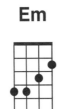	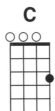	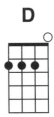	

Baritone Ukulele

G	Em	C	D
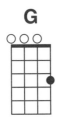	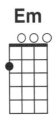	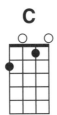	

Guitar

G	Em	C	D
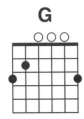	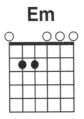	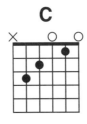	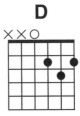

Mandolin

G	Em	C	D

Banjo

G	Em	C	D
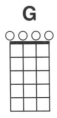	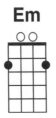		

Stand by Me

Words and Music by Jerry Leiber, Mike Stoller and Ben E. King

Standard Ukulele

E	G	D	A	Am7	Bm7	Em7	B7sus4

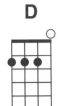
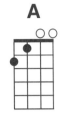
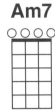

Baritone Ukulele

E	G	D	A	Am7	Bm7	Em7	B7sus4

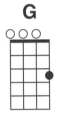

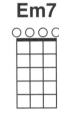
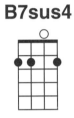

Guitar

E	G	D	A	Am7	Bm7	Em7	B7sus4

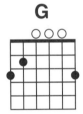

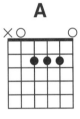
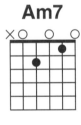

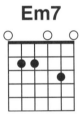

Mandolin

E	G	D	A	Am7	Bm7	Em7	B7sus4

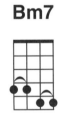

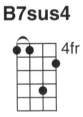

Banjo

E	G	D	A	Am7	Bm7	Em7	B7sus4

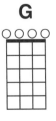

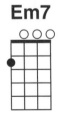
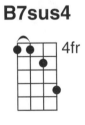

Summer Breeze
Words and Music by James Seals and Dash Crofts

Standard Ukulele

G	D	C	F
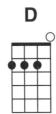	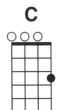	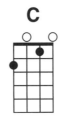	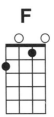

Baritone Ukulele

G	D	C	F
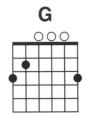	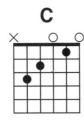	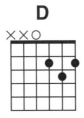	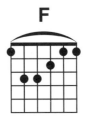

Guitar

G	D	C	F
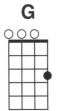		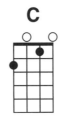	

Mandolin

G	D	C	F
		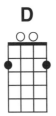	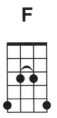

Banjo

G	D	C	F
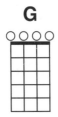	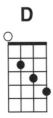	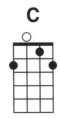	

Sundown

Words and Music by Gordon Lightfoot

Standard Ukulele

G	C	Am7	D7	Bm

Baritone Ukulele

G	C	Am7	D7	Bm

Guitar

G	C	Am7	D7	Bm

Mandolin

G	C	Am7	D7	Bm
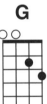				

Banjo

G	C	Am7	D7	Bm

Sunshine on My Shoulders

Words by John Denver
Music by John Denver, Mike Taylor and Dick Kniss

Standard Ukulele

C
F
G
C6
G7
Em
Dm

Baritone Ukulele

C
F
G
C6
G7
Em
Dm

Guitar

C
F
G
C6
G7
Em
Dm

Mandolin

C
F
G
C6
G7
Em
Dm

Banjo

C
F
G
C6
5fr
G7
Em
Dm

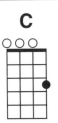

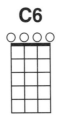

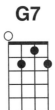

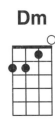

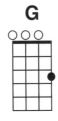

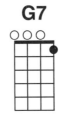

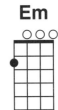

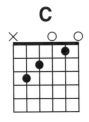

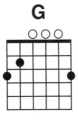

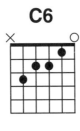

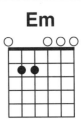

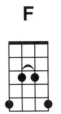

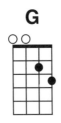

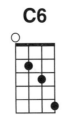

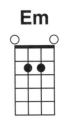

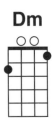

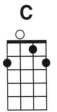

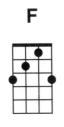

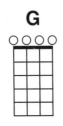

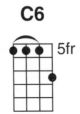

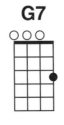

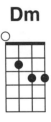

Sweet Caroline
Words and Music by Neil Diamond

Standard Ukulele

Em	C	Bsus4	B	Am	Em7	A7

Baritone Ukulele

Em	C	Bsus4	B	Am	Em7	A7

Guitar

Em	C	Bsus4	B	Am	Em7	A7

Mandolin

Em	C	Bsus4	B	Am	Em7	A7

Banjo

Em	C	Bsus4	B	Am	Em7	A7

Sweet Dreams (Are Made of This)

Words and Music by Annie Lennox and David Stewart

Standard Ukulele

D	C	G	F
	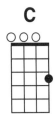	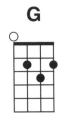	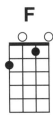

Baritone Ukulele

D	C	G	F
	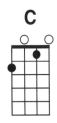	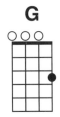	

Guitar

D	C	G	F
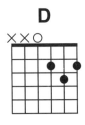	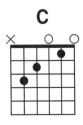	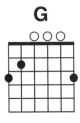	

Mandolin

D	C	G	F
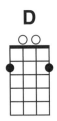		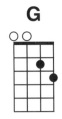	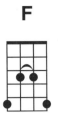

Banjo

D	C	G	F
	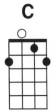	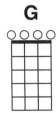	

Sweet Home Alabama

Words and Music by Ronnie Van Zant, Ed King and Gary Rossington

Additional Lyrics

2. Well, I heard Mister Young sing about her.
Well, I heard ole Neil put her down.
Well, I hope Neil Young will remember
A Southern man don't need him around anyhow.

3. In Birmingham they love the gov'nor, boo-hoo-hoo.
Now, we all did what we could do.
Now, Watergate does not bother me.
Does your conscience bother you? Tell the truth.

4. Now, Muscle Shoals has got the Swampers,
And they've been known to pick a song or two.
Lord, they get me off so much.
They pick me up when I'm feeling blue. Now how 'bout you?

Standard Ukulele

G	Em	D	C	F

Baritone Ukulele

G	Em	D	C	F

Guitar

G	Em	D	C	F
			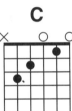	

Mandolin

G	Em	D	C	F
		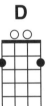		

Banjo

G	Em	D	C	F

Take Me Home, Country Roads

Words and Music by John Denver, Bill Danoff and Taffy Nivert

Standard Ukulele

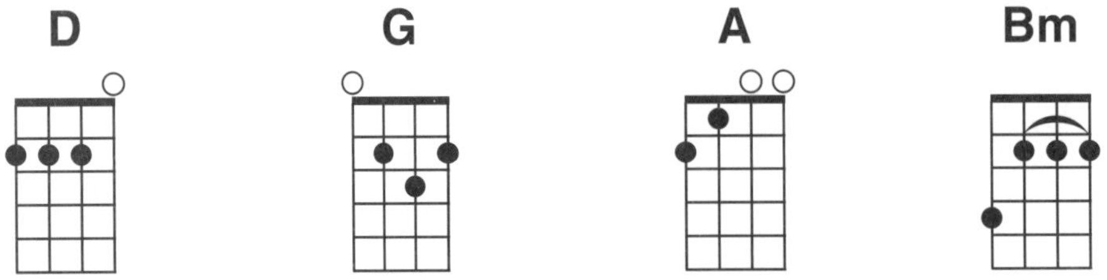
D
G
A
Bm

Baritone Ukulele

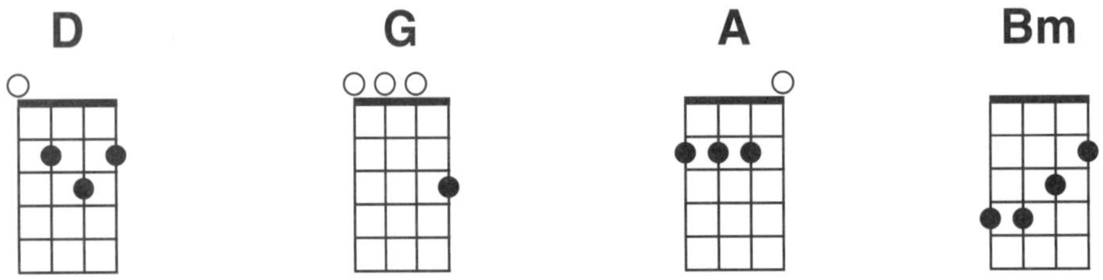
D
G
A
Bm

Guitar

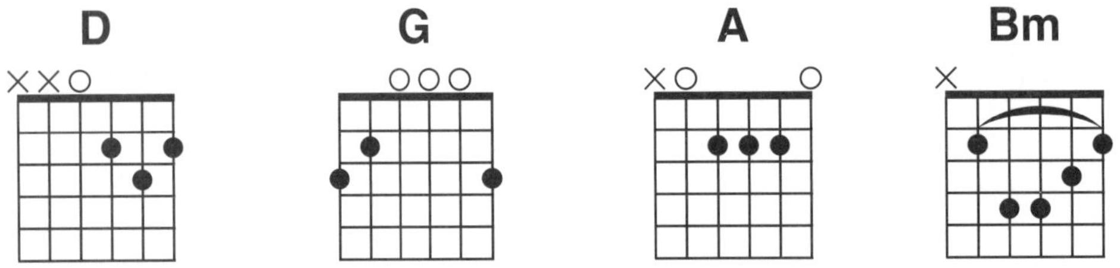
D
G
A
Bm

Mandolin

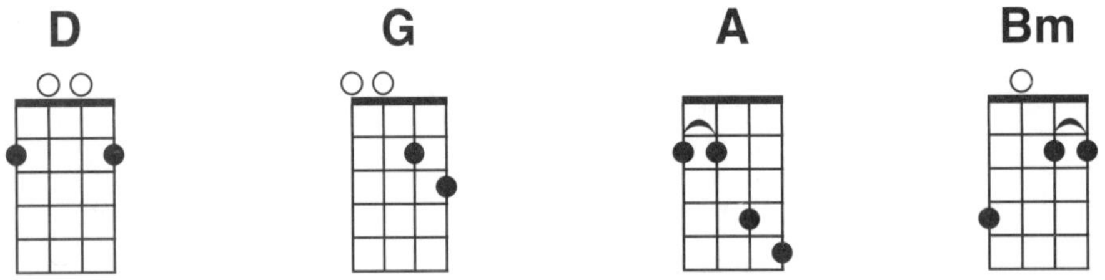
D
G
A
Bm

Banjo

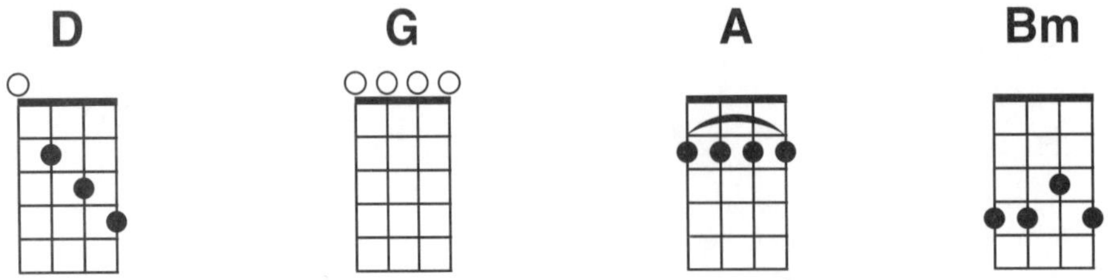
D
G
A
Bm

Teach Your Children

Words and Music by Graham Nash

Standard Ukulele

G	D	A
		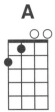

Baritone Ukulele

G	D	A
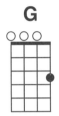	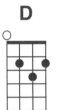	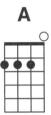

Guitar

G	D	A
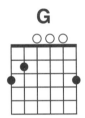	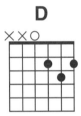	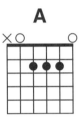

Mandolin

G	D	A
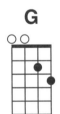	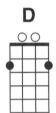	

Banjo

G	D	A
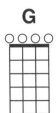		

This Land Is Your Land

Words and Music by Woody Guthrie

Standard Ukulele

A	D	E
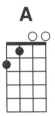	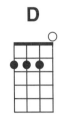	

Baritone Ukulele

A	D	E

Guitar

A	D	E
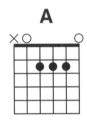	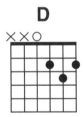	

Mandolin

A	D	E
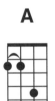	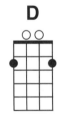	

Banjo

A	D	E

Three Little Birds

Words and Music by Bob Marley

Standard Ukulele

C	Am	F	G7	Dm

Baritone Ukulele

C	Am	F	G7	Dm

Guitar

C	Am	F	G7	Dm

Mandolin

C	Am	F	G7	Dm

Banjo

C	Am	F	G7	Dm

Where Have All the Flowers Gone?

Words and Music by Pete Seeger

Verse
Moderately

1. Where have all the flow - ers gone, _ long time
2. Where have all the young girls gone, _ long time
3. Where have all the young men gone, _ long time
4. Where have all the sol - diers gone, _ long time
5. Where have all the grave - yards gone, _ long time

pass - ing? _ Where have all the flow - ers gone, _____
pass - ing? _ Where have all the young girls gone, _____
pass - ing? _ Where have all the young men gone, _____
pass - ing? _ Where have all the sol - diers gone, _____
pass - ing? _ Where have all the grave - yards gone. _____

long time a - go? Where have all the
long time a - go? Where have all the
long time a - go? Where have all the
long time a - go? Where have all the
long time a - go? Where have all the

flow - ers gone? _ Young girls picked them, ev - 'ry one. _
young girls gone? _ Gone to young men, ev - 'ry one. _
young men gone? _ Gone for sol - diers, ev - 'ry one. _
sol - diers gone? _ Gone to grave - yards, ev - 'ry one. _
grave - yards gone? _ Gone to flow - ers, ev - 'ry one. _

When will they ev - er learn? _ When will they ev - er

1.–4.
learn?

5.
learn?

Standard Ukulele

| G | F#m7 | B7 | Em | C | D | A |

Baritone Ukulele

| G | F#m7 | B7 | Em | C | D | A |

     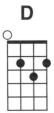

Guitar

| G | F#m7 | B7 | Em | C | D | A |

Mandolin

| G | F#m7 | B7 | Em | C | D | A |

     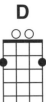

Banjo

| G | F#m7 | B7 | Em | C | D | A |

Yesterday
Words and Music by John Lennon and Paul McCartney

Standard Ukulele

A	D	E7
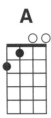	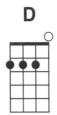	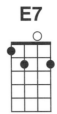

Baritone Ukulele

A	D	E7
	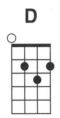	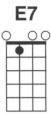

Guitar

A	D	E7
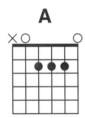	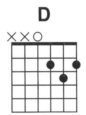	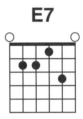

Mandolin

A	D	E7
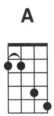	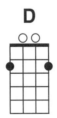	

Banjo

A	D	E7
		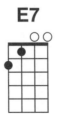

You Are My Sunshine
Words and Music by Jimmie Davis

Standard Ukulele

Em	C	D	Bm	G	Am

Baritone Ukulele

Em	C	D	Bm	G	Am

Guitar

Em	C	D	Bm	G	Am

Mandolin

Em	C	D	Bm	G	Am

 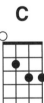  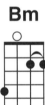 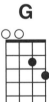

Banjo

Em	C	D	Bm	G	Am

You're So Vain

Words and Music by Carly Simon

Tuning

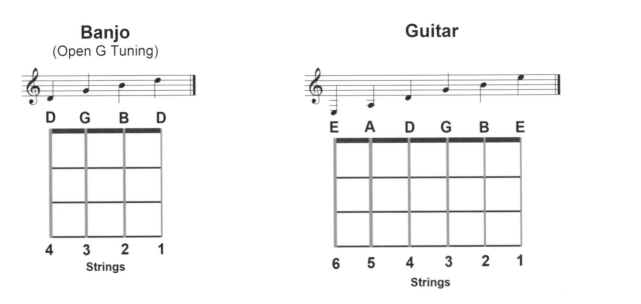

All banjo chord formations illustrated in this book are based on "Open G" tuning. If an alternate tuning is used the banjo player can read the chord letters for the songs and disregard the diagrams.